STAY WORRY-FREE
WITH EPICTETUS

Jana Capri lives in Barcelona, Spain, speaks five languages and holds a degree in Translation and Interpretation from Charles University in Prague. She is a Master Practitioner in NLP (Neuro-Linguistic Programming) and has studied psychological astrology and creative writing. Jana is also a blogger and co-author of several books.

She has a strong interest in psychosomatics and personal growth and enjoys reading and writing books that inspire self-improvement and help others feel better about themselves.

Charan Díaz Arquillo is a psychologist based in Barcelona, Spain, with over twenty years of experience in psychotherapy, personal growth, educational psychology and organisational psychology. He holds a master's degree in Humanistic and Integrative Psychotherapy, as well as certifications in Mindfulness and Clinical Hypnosis from the University of Barcelona. Charan is also an author and co-author of several books.

He is passionate about Hindu and Greek philosophy, as well as oriental tales and mythology.

JANA CAPRI AND CHARAN DÍAZ

STAY WORRY-FREE

WITH EPICTETUS

79 QUESTIONS AND ANSWERS FROM STOIC PHILOSOPHY

Published by Westland Books, a division of Nasadiya Technologies Private Limited, in 2025

No. 269/2B, First Floor, 'Irai Arul', Vimalraj Street, Nethaji Nagar, Alapakkam Main Road, Maduravoyal, Chennai 600095

Westland and the Westland logo are the trademarks of Nasadiya Technologies Private Limited, or its affiliates.

This English edition for the Indian Subcontinent published by arrangement with Suasive Consultants Private Limited (www.montsecortazar.com). Jana Capri and Charan Díaz assert the moral right to be identified as the authors of this work.

ISBN: 9789360452162

10 9 8 7 6 5 4 3

The views and opinions expressed in this work are the authors' own and the facts are as reported by them, and the publisher is in no way liable for the same.

Typeset by Jojy Philip

Printed at Thomson Press India Private Limited

CONTENTS

INTRODUCTION

Close your eyes and assume a comfortable posture. Take a few deep breaths and let your body relax completely. While you are doing this, ask yourself: what is stopping me from being well and happy right now? What could jeopardise my joy in the coming days and weeks?

What will come to your mind will probably be some kind of **concern.** It could be your financial situation, the health of a family member, or maybe you're just worried about your empty fridge and wondering what you're going to eat tonight.

Whatever it is, the vast majority of people in this world will have some worries on their mind at any given moment. It is estimated that we have around 60,000 thoughts a day, and most of these are negative and tinged with anxiety, fear or anger.

For a rational mind like ours, which is capable of thinking abstractly and visualising the future, worry is near impossible to avoid. What is possible, however, is to analyse these worries and see how important they are and how we can feel better about them.

And this is where the **Stoics** come in. Stoic philosophy is a key that can free us. It teaches us how to cope with the ups and downs in life better and, consequently, improve the quality of our existence.

In this book, we will see how **Epictetus,** a slave who became one of the greatest Stoics in humanity, thinks about issues that remain as relevant today as it was in his time.

What affects you is not what happens to you, but your interpretation of what has happened to you.

This is a Stoic maxim of Epictetus that a psychologist might tell their clients. The philosopher tells us that what happens is something objective, but we decide how we react to it.

Epictetus (c. 50–135 CE) lived a part of his life as a slave in Rome. He managed to attend lectures given by Musonius Rufus, a Roman senator and Stoic philosopher, before becoming a freedman. Epictetus soon discovered that beyond physical slavery, what makes us suffer daily is our 'mental slavery'. We still suffer from this slavery today, when we lose our temper, become irrational or have a negative attitude.

And although on one hand, physical slavery and the circumstances of his time were harsh and very different from our modern day, on the other, mental worries were similar to those we have today. That is, they suffered from fear of the future, fretted about economic problems, compared themselves with others, endured criticism from loved ones, worried about death, futilely desisted accepting the inevitable, etc., just like we do.

The intention of this book is to bring Epictetus and a selection of his **inspirational teachings** closer to you, the reader. The book will give answers to current problems, and it will be as if you were having a coffee with the Stoic and he was your friend, your psychologist or your mentor. His answers will be accompanied by a brief psychological reflection.

Epictetus' answers are all inspired by the original work quoted. They are not always verbatim **quotations** but are adapted for easier understanding. In a dialogue format with his interlocutor, this wise man comes alive for the reader and it becomes easier to learn from him, identify with the conversation and remember his wisdom in the future.

We wish you a happy psychological-philosophical journey, where you will feel less worried in the company of Epictetus. If at least one of his ideas inspires you to find greater serenity at some point in your life, then the time and attention devoted to this book will have been well worth it.

HOW TO USE THIS BOOK

If you have read our books *Stay Calm with Seneca* or *Stay Positive with Marcus Aurelius*, you will see that we have followed a similar format.

On the next page, we explain the three parts of each chapter: (1) a question or comment from a seeker, (2) Epictetus' answer and (3) a psychological reflection.

By 'seeker' we mean all those who ask themselves questions about the mysteries of life and want to get answers based on this everlasting wisdom.

Epictetus' answers are inspired by his teachings, recorded in *The Enchiridion* and *The Handbook and Maxims*, both published by his student Arrian. The responses are specially selected to deal with worries and concerns, and adapted to modern language for easy understanding.

The subsequent psychological reflection is food for thought, aiming to guide further deliberation on Epictetus' messages. These suggested viewpoints should not be considered instructions or definitive interpretations of the Stoic messages, but rather invitations for the reader to pose questions and to consider elements that might help them integrate the Stoic approach into their life.

1

DON'T BLAME ANYONE

Question/comment from a seeker:

When I have a bad day, I find myself blaming and criticising others, and then feeling bad about my actions. What would a wise man do in such situations?

Epictetus' Answer (The Enchiridion–Chapter V):

The ignorant person blames others for what goes wrong in their life; the one who has begun to learn philosophy blames only themselves; but a truly wise person blames neither others nor themselves.

DON'T BLAME ANYONE 3

Psychological Reflection

When things don't go as expected, we tend to look for a culprit, a scapegoat. In such difficult moments, a person's maturity is often put to the test.

Many adults react like children when something frustrates them. Imagine a couple who have bought tickets to the movies. On their way to the cinema, they run into a traffic jam and realise that they will not make it on time. Then, one of them starts to accuse the other of leaving home late, while the other complains that they had wanted to see another film but had gone along with their partner to avoid disagreements and now they feel they have lost their money, and so on.

A person who is interested in personal growth, and understands that life is a school, will know that instead of blaming the other person, he or she should take their share of the responsibility and focus on their learning.

According to Epictetus, the wise person accepts fate, knowing that there is no point in blaming anyone for anything that happens in life. But at the same time, the wise person is aware of what depends on them and always does the best he or she can.

Question or comment about life.

The answer inspired by Epictetus' *The Enchiridion* and curated thoughts from his *Discourses,* as presented in *Manual y Máximas* [*The Handbook and Maxims*]. The reference to the corresponding text is in brackets.

Psychological reflection to explore the message in more depth.

HOW TO GET THE MOST OUT OF THIS BOOK

We recommend that you use this book whenever:

- You are going through a difficult period in your life.
- You want to reduce your level of anxiety.
- You need more peace of mind.
- You want to relieve worries, stress, etc.
- You are looking for inspiration.

You can select from the contents the chapter name that inspires you the most, or open the book at random and see which message you land upon.

The great sages and philosophers of human history such as Seneca, Marcus Aurelius, Socrates, Epictetus and the Buddha help us understand that cultivating the desired attitude is not a matter of days, months or years, but rather a lifelong work.

Despite this, it is worth the effort.

1

DON'T BLAME ANYONE

Question/comment from a seeker:

When I have a bad day, I find myself blaming and criticising others, and then feeling bad about my actions. What would a wise man do in such situations?

Epictetus' answer (*The Enchiridion,* Chapter V):

The ignorant person blames others for what goes wrong in their life; the one who has begun to learn philosophy blames only themselves; but a truly wise person blames neither others nor themselves.

Psychological Reflection

When things don't go as expected, we tend to look for a culprit, a scapegoat. In such difficult moments, a person's maturity is often put to the test.

Many adults react like children when something frustrates them. Imagine a couple who have bought tickets to the movies. On their way to the cinema, they run into a traffic jam and realise that they will not make it on time. Then, one of them starts to accuse the other of leaving home late, while the other complains that they had wanted to see another film but had gone along with their partner to avoid disagreements and now they feel they have lost their money, and so on.

A person who is interested in personal growth, and understands that life is a school, will know that instead of blaming the other person, he or she should take their share of the responsibility and focus on their learning.

According to Epictetus, the wise person accepts fate, knowing that there is no point in blaming anyone for anything that happens in life. But at the same time, the wise person is aware of what depends on them and always does the best he or she can.

2

LOVE YOUR REALITY

Question/comment from a seeker:

My life isn't going well right now despite my efforts. There are many things in my private life and at work that don't go as planned, and this causes me a lot of stress.

Epictetus' answer (*The Enchiridion*, Chapter VIII):

Don't expect that things will happen as you would like them to. If you wish to feel good, learn to like and be at peace with whatever happens to you.

Psychological Reflection

Let's imagine the thoughts of a person who is going on a holiday: *I want to see this, I want to experience that, I will go to that restaurant and eat that dessert, I will go to that park with the great reviews and it will be fantastic there.* This person is in love with this idealistic holiday they have built in their mind. But what if it doesn't go as expected? They will probably end up disappointed and frustrated because the reality falls short of their imagination.

What would Epictetus tell us in such a situation? We need to be more open-minded and flexible, and learn to enjoy what life has to offer. Satisfaction does not depend so much on what happens as it does on how you respond to it.

The ability to improvise creatively and adapt to reality when things are not as we expected is a sign of personal maturity. We often suffer because we resist 'loving what is'.

3

WHAT DEPENDS ON YOU

Question/comment from a seeker:

Sometimes, I get frustrated and depressed about things I can't change. How can I better differentiate between things that depend on me and those that don't?

Epictetus' answer (*The Enchiridion*, Chapter I):

There are very few things that actually depend on us: our interpretation of what happens, our willingness to take action, what we desire and what we are prepared to reject.

In short, all our actions depend on us. But our body, wealth, reputation, position of power—in other words, anything that is beyond our actions—do not depend on us.

Psychological Reflection

To be free, we first need to recognise what our freedom consists of and to what extent we can control what happens to us.

According to the Stoics, we always have the freedom and power to choose what we do with what happens to us, that is, how we respond to the challenges of destiny. Our opinions, actions, likes and dislikes are entirely within our control.

To paraphrase the psychotherapist Ana Gimeno Bayon, 'I don't choose the colour of my eyes or my height, but I can choose how I dress, how I take care of my body.'

And what about our inner world? Do we choose our feelings? No, but we are free to choose what we *do* with our feelings. If you feel bad, you can go for a walk, take a hot bath and do some relaxation exercises. Or you can choose to abuse everyone who crosses your path and blame them for your bad day. It's up to you how you act, and that's what your freedom is all about.

On the other hand, almost everything else in life is beyond our control. They are dependent on external factors and cannot be relied upon to follow a favourable course. With the acceptance of our lack of say in these things comes peace of mind.

If you're worried about a problem, remember that you are free in many ways: you can choose how you interpret the issue and how you go about resolving it.

4

ASSESS YOUR ABILITIES WELL

Question/comment from a seeker:

I am not good at my job and I lack enthusiasm for it.

Epictetus' answer (*The Enchiridion*, Chapter XXXVII):

If you don't assess your capabilities correctly, you may end up being overwhelmed doing something you are not good at and, at the same time, miss the opportunity to make use of your strengths where you could have made a good impact.

Psychological Reflection

The tiger, no matter how good a swimmer, will never swim like the shark. The tiger moves better on land, its natural environment. Epictetus advises us to make a self-assessment so that we spend our time and make our efforts wisely.

This does not mean that we should all look for the job of our dreams and never settle for a 'normal' career. Depending on the situation we find ourselves in, a boring job that pays the bills can be a smart decision. We simply need to take a good look at why we do what we do—what the reasons are and whether our choice is a good one, taking into account all the necessary factors.

Do you feel like a tiger stuck treading water at your current job? What can you do to make sure your skills and abilities fit your present role better? Can you think of some other work you would excel at? What steps do you need to take in order to switch careers?

5

YOU'RE READY TO FACE ANYTHING

Question/comment from a seeker:

There are days when I'm just not able to cope with my problems.

Epictetus' answer (*Maxims*, Of Religion and Gods, 22):

God has provided you with weapons necessary to face the toughest situations.

These weapons are, among others, the greatness of your soul, the strength of your will, and your patience and perseverance. Use them, and if you don't, at least have the awareness that you are ignoring assets that can make you very powerful.

Psychological Reflection

According to the Stoics, everything we require to have a good life is within us. With just our virtues and our strengths, we are already sufficiently equipped for any battle that life throws at us. These 'weapons' are God's gift to mankind, and we must make good use of them.

It is not always easy, of course. We are not in the best of spirits always and sometimes, we may not find the strength to face the ups and downs in our day-to-day lives. And that's fine, we are all human beings and as such, are entitled to have a bad day or a bad time. What Epictetus wants to remind us with this quote is that we are prepared, we are 'equipped' for those days of inner rain, and that if we have faith and confidence in our ability to solve life's problems, we will manage to do so.

Think of a current challenge and ask yourself: what weapons do I have that can help me emerge from this battle with my head held high? Will it be my patience, my perseverance, my kindness or my caution? Perhaps it is all of them.

6

FIND YOUR PERSONAL POWER

Question/comment from a seeker:

What advice would you give me so that I can be more empowered in life?

Epictetus' answer (*The Enchiridion*, Chapter X):

No matter what happens, find out what power you possess within yourself to make the situation beneficial to you.

If you feel lazy or tired, the power you have is your strength of will; if you are insulted or offended, the power you can practise is patience. If you get used to responding to all situations with your powers, you will no longer be trapped by worries and negative thoughts.

Psychological Reflection

People who are obsessed with the question, 'What will happen to me now?' tend to imagine possible threats and experience greater anxiety when going through a personal crisis (divorce, dismissal from the workplace, family problems, etc.).

But people who ask themselves, 'What can I do on my part to be OK?' or 'What power do I have that can help me deal with this situation better?' during a difficult predicament, cope much better because they have a growth mindset and focus on the solution.

Think about a situation that is currently troubling you. What personal power do you have to make it easier for you to benefit from this set of circumstances in some way?

7

INNER FREEDOM

Question/comment from a seeker:

How can I be freer in life?

Epictetus' answer (*The Enchiridion*, Chapter XIV):

When a person seeks freedom, they no longer desire or try to avoid things that depend on others; for if they do so, they remain a slave.

Psychological Reflection

How much energy do we waste trying to convince others of something or attempting to make things happen that are not up to us? How much effort expended in vain, trying to avoid the unpleasant things that we can't control?

How would all your worries change if you only focused on what is up to you? Wouldn't you have more inner freedom? Psychological freedom and independence can be developed. Epictetus gives us a clear advice: to make more conscious decisions and be able to live better with what we have today, we have to focus only on what depends on us.

8

DO YOU ASSERT YOURSELF?

Question/comment from a seeker:

I find it difficult to say no to others. Consequently, I end up overwhelmed and stressed because I take on more than I can handle, particularly at my job.

Epictetus' answer (*Maxims*, Of Self-improvement, 27):

Every person sets their price—high or low, according to their perception—and every person is worth what they *make* themselves worth. Choose then, whether you will behave like a slave or like a free person. It's up to you.

Psychological Reflection

Our perception, or the image we have of ourselves, influences us in all areas of our lives, whether it is love, work, family or friendship. The way we see ourselves is directly related to the confidence we have in our values and resources and this, in turn, affects our relationships with other people.

In situations where too much is demanded of us, we need to think about how we can self-regulate to stay well. Because if you don't take care of yourself, you won't be a good worker, friend or partner. As the flight safety instructions go, we need to put our own mask on first before helping others.

Do you act and behave as if your well-being is important no matter the situation, or do you yield to others' demands and find it difficult to set boundaries? In what contexts and why?

9

BE LIKE HERCULES

Question/comment from a seeker:

Why is life so complicated and why do we have to face so many difficulties?

Epictetus' answer (*Maxims*, Of Self-improvement, 38):

Would Hercules have been Hercules without the lion, boar, Hydra, Cerberus, and other monsters and criminals he liberated the world from? And if not for these challenges, what would have been the use of his muscular arms, his enormous strength, his bravery, his unflappable determination and the rest of his virtues?

Psychological Reflection

A toxic boss, a demanding partner, a contentious neighbour, a society without values ... there will always be 'monsters' in our life. How do we deal with them? This decision will bring us closer to or take us farther away from the kind of person we want to be and the kind of life we aspire to have. The way we deal with these everyday challenges makes us who we are.

Think of a current 'monster' in your life that worries you. What resources do you have, or can you obtain (by asking for help, learning something …) to be able to face it with dignity and wisdom?

10

ACCEPT GOD'S WILL

Question/comment from a seeker:

Am I a conformist if I accept everything that happens in my life, even if it is bad?

Epictetus' answer (*The Enchiridion*, Chapter LIII):

Always keep this in mind: if this is God's will, so be it. Everything is OK.

Psychological Reflection

Which is better: accepting things as they are or fighting to change them? To decide, we first have to look at the issue and ask ourselves whether it is in our hands.

If the answer is 'it's not up to me', then why get angry and resentful, or fight against something you can't change? The best attitude is acceptance: calm down, get over it and channel your energy into something more useful.

On the other hand, if the answer is 'yes, this is up to me', the best thing to do is determine how you will deal with it, and take action.

Think about a current situation that you find difficult to accept but cannot change. What can you do to come to terms with the circumstances? If you find it hard to make peace with what is happening, how long are you willing to fight against something that doesn't depend on you?

11

BAD HABITS

Question/comment from a seeker:

I have bad habits that I find hard to break.

Epictetus' answer (*Maxims*, Of Self-improvement, 68):

Bad habits can only be replaced by consistently practising good habits. If you have become accustomed to being very materialistic, you will have to master it by practising austerity. If you live a lazy life, you will have to work. If you are very irritable, learn to suffer criticisms with patience. And if you follow this advice with all your other harmful habits, you will very soon realise that your efforts have been worthwhile.

Psychological Reflection

Think of a bad habit you currently have that you would like to break.

What would be the opposite habit?

When would you be willing to start practising that healthier habit to feel better?

12

HELPING OTHERS

Question/comment from a seeker:

Should we help someone who needs it but has not asked for it?

Epictetus' answer (*Maxims*, Of Self-improvement, 80):

No one has to beg the sun to give everyone its light and warmth. Likewise, be as good as you can be to others without waiting to be asked.

Psychological Reflection

Stoics remind us that for human beings, using your feet to walk is as natural as being kind.

Think back to the last time you received help from someone you didn't expect. How did it make you feel?

Now recall a time when you helped someone without the person expecting it. How did you come to the decision to help them? What assistance did you provide? How did it make you feel? Is there someone in your life right now who could use your help?

13

NOT EVERYTHING IS BLACK OR WHITE

Question/comment from a seeker:

I've had some health problems lately and I find it hard to keep my spirits up when I'm not feeling well.

Epictetus' answer (*Maxims*, Of the Deceptive Opinion of Things, 23):

Believing that health is always a good thing and illness is always a bad thing is wrong.

What matters is what you do with your health—if you treat your body well, it is good; if you abuse it, it is bad.

It is the same with illness; the crucial factor is what you do with what you have been given. There is good to be found in everything.

Psychological Reflection

Life is like a game—sometimes we are dealt a good hand, and sometimes we aren't. We can have good cards (good health) and play a bad game (spoil it), and we can also have bad cards (illness) and play as strategically as possible (take care of ourselves as best we can, accept what we can't change, and handle the illness with dignity).

How much of your illness, pain or discomfort is in your control? When you fight against something you cannot change, it only increases your suffering.

If, for example, you suffer from chronic pain, you may have to accept that this is what you have been dealt (bad cards) and that you cannot avoid feeling pain. If you resist pain, preoccupied as you are with battling your illness, your discomfort will only increase. Now, there are many things you can do to feel better—learn pain management techniques, indulge in pleasant or relaxing activities, think of all the things you can do despite your suffering, etc.

Epictetus reminds us that not everything is black and white. Once we analyse what is in our hands and what is not, and then concentrate only on what we can control, we will have made the best use of this Stoic maxim.

14

THE PRICE OF ANGER

Question/comment from a seeker:

When someone criticises me or treats me unfairly, I usually respond very badly. I can't stand it.

Epictetus' answer (*The Enchiridion*, Chapter XX):

When you get angry because of another person, realise that your thoughts are fuelling the inner flames of fury. At that moment, it would be better not to let yourself be carried away by what you think. Rather, put the whole thing off and buy yourself some time so that you can keep your cool.

Psychological Reflection

What is the price we pay if we are driven by anger? Anger harms us in the following ways:

It worsens relationships with loved ones, friends and co-workers.

It further complicates the original situation or problem.

It stresses our body.

It makes us think negatively, we feel guilty, and life seems much worse than it is.

Next time you get angry, try to put off the issue until you are calmer and more objective, and you will be able to look at everything with a friendlier gaze.

15

IS IT WORTH IT?

Question/comment from a seeker:

How can I be happy if I don't have a loving partner, a good job or good health? These are basic things that everyone needs to be happy.

Epictetus' answer (*Maxims*, Of Freedom and Slavery, 6):

Do you think you would be happy if all your wishes came true? You are very wrong, my friend! As soon as you have what you so desire, you would be a victim; not only of that which you yearned for, but also of new worries, fears and desires. Happiness does not come from acquiring more and more and enjoying those things, but rather, it is about not wanting anything and being at ease with the prospect of going without. This is what it means to be truly free.

Psychological Reflection

One of the ideas that Epictetus frequently repeats is that we should reduce our desires to a minimum. Desire, for him, is a bottomless pit—it never ends, and as soon as one desire has been fulfilled, we have already set our eyes on the next, thinking that the new target will finally make us happy.

But according to the Stoics, when our wish comes true, what we experience is not real happiness. And not only that, from the moment the wish is created until it is realised, many unpleasant things happen—we feel anxious about the chances of attaining it, fear that our hopes may not be fulfilled, and we blame any situation or person that stands in the way of satisfying our wants.

The next time we get excited about something, we should ask ourselves: is it worth it? What price am I paying to get what I want so badly? How would I feel if I didn't have this desire—would I be more relaxed?

16

SHOW EMPATHY BUT WITH LIMITS

Question/comment from a seeker:

It affects me a lot when I see a loved one having a hard time. Should I have a more detached attitude?

Epictetus' answer (*The Enchiridion*, Chapter XVI):

When you see someone grieving for a loved one or for the loss of anything they owned, do not think that the cause of their suffering is something external. Remember that it is not what has happened to them that affects them, but their interpretation of what has happened to them.

Even so, show your compassion and empathy and, if necessary, accompany them in mourning their loss. But be careful not to let it get to you too deeply.

Psychological Reflection

Suffering is not something objective and external that can be gauged with a tape measure, but rather something subjective, which depends on how we look at it. Two people can experience the same situation but not react to it in the same way, because no two minds are the same, and their perspectives can be quite different.

Modern psychology confirms what Epictetus expressed centuries ago: what affects us emotionally depends on our interpretation of what is happening. Our inner dialogue, the explanations we give ourselves and the conclusions we come to when something happens, all make a difference in the intensity of emotional pain.

Epictetus advises us to have empathy and compassion for the person who is suffering. You should never try to lecture or give advice to people while they are in pain. But the Stoic suggests empathy without being consumed with the other person's pain. A doctor should be compassionate with the patient, but not to the point where they can no longer operate, because then they become part of the problem and not part of the solution.

17

HOW TO MAKE DECISIONS

Question/comment from a seeker:

When it comes to jobs and partners, I'm like a butterfly going from flower to flower. I don't like anyone or anything, and I'm afraid to commit myself.

Epictetus' answer (*The Enchiridion*, Chapter XXIX):

Before you act, analyse everything very well. If you don't do this, you will always start in high spirits without worrying, but when difficulties arise, you will give up too easily and end up embarrassed.

Psychological Reflection

Before making an important decision, it is worth deliberating a little first. Some people get too caught up in wishful thinking without any prior analysis of reality. For example, when we have to choose between several careers or jobs, we can ask ourselves these questions: *how do I see myself doing in this job? Does it align with my strengths and what I am good at? Is it smart to pursue this in the mid- and long-term? Do I like it and does it motivate me? Does it fit with my values?*

When we have analysed and concluded what feels right, what we want to do and what is the smart thing to do, then we have to have the courage to take the leap, commit to that choice and 'make it ours'.

Are you holding back from something you want to do? Is there an important change you know you need to make? What is it that you need in order to take action: more reasoning, more courage or more commitment?

18

NOTHING IS FREE

Question/comment from a seeker:

At my age, I should have achieved many more things. Am I too passive? Is that why I feel stuck in life?

Epictetus' answer (*The Enchiridion*, Chapter XXV):

Would it be logical that someone who never knocks on the door gets the same response as someone who constantly does? Will the person who never compliments anyone be as appreciated as the one who does?

You are very unreasonable if you expect to get things without paying the cost.

Psychological Reflection

Epictetus advises us not to expect to get anything for free, or without taking any action.

How many interviews did you attend before you got a good job?

How many dates did you go on before having a formal partner?

How many sleepless nights did you have when your child was born?

How long did you have to work for before you could become a bit more independent?

How many years did you meditate before you could appreciate the benefits of meditation?

Every achievement has its price and there is always something we can do to get closer to our goal. Whether we get what we want depends on destiny, but either way, we will have to do our part.

What 'price' do you think you should pay to get closer to the achievements that are not yet in your hands?

19

THE REAL VICTORY

Question/comment from a seeker:

Although I have been successful in some areas of my life, I am not happy. Why is happiness so complicated?

Epictetus' answer (*Maxims*, Of Own Perfection, 74):

Neither victory in the Olympic Games nor glory in war can make a human being happy. The only triumphs that you truly achieve are the ones you win against yourself. Temptations and setbacks are the real inner war.

Have you lost one battle, two or three? Keep fighting. If you finally win in that inner war, you will be happy all your life, and it will be as if you had always won.

Psychological Reflection

When did we learn in our education to seek happiness within ourselves without depending on external influences? Never, since no one teaches us this. These are questions that often don't interest us until we hit rock bottom and have a really bad time.

The person who only strives for external and material things is forgetting the essence of their life, the quality of their inner world. But wherever you go, your heart accompanies you twenty-four hours a day, seven days a week. And if your heart is not well, you cannot be well.

How much time do you spend a week managing your emotions, thoughts and spiritual needs to win your inner civil war and become happier?

20

ACCEPT WHAT IS

Question/comment from a seeker:

What is freedom? What can I do to gain more freedom?

Epictetus' answer (*Maxims*, Of Liberty and Slavery, 5):

Freedom is not only beautiful but also very reasonable. That's why you will understand that it is absurd and irrational to wish for many things and to expect everything to go according to our plans. If, for instance, I write the word 'God', I will have to write it as it is, letter by letter (G-O-D), and not just in any way I want to; the same applies to all sciences and arts.

Stop fooling yourself, my friend. Real freedom is won by accepting and wanting everything that happens exactly as it is, irrespective of whether it matches your likes and inclinations.

Psychological Reflection

Sometimes we believe that being free is always doing what we like, not following rules and having no limits. But the Stoics tell us that this is a naïve point of view.

If you love freedom, you stop expecting everything to happen according to your plans and you understand that life has its own designs. To be free is to accept the things that are not in our hands. If we have many hopes and wishes, we cease to be free, because we get irritated and angry when these are not fulfilled. Are we really free if we depend on the realisation of our desires to feel good?

Are you able to love who you are and adapt to your reality? How do you react when your expectations and desires are not met? How can you achieve freedom in this sense?

21

DON'T LOSE YOUR NERVE

Question/comment from a seeker:

I get nervous when I forget something drop something or have small accidents. Even if they are sometimes trivial, I don't know how to keep calm.

Epictetus' answer (*The Enchiridion*, Chapter XII):

It begins with the small things. Has the oil spilled? Has your wine been stolen? You can overcome it all by saying to yourself, 'This is the price I pay to keep calm, this is the cost of serenity,' because you won't get something for nothing.

Psychological Reflection

Every time our toast is burnt, we miss the bus, a client is upset, a colleague at work criticises us or our smartphone is stolen, take inspiration from this wisdom of Epictetus. If we develop tolerance and breathe easy even with the small discomforts in everyday life, we will be better able to tolerate other major stress factors in the future (such as a layoff, a divorce, a change of apartment, etc.).

Once we train our self-control with the small setbacks, then we can deal with the bigger ones better.

When was the last time your dinner was burnt and you took it easy? Will you be able to stop, breathe and think of something nicer the next time a little setback happens?

22

FEAR

Question/comment from a seeker:

I admit that I have many fears: fear of getting sick, of losing my job, of losing my partner, of not knowing where life will take me ...

Epictetus' answer (*Maxims*, Miscellaneous, 31):

You don't have to be afraid of poverty, prison or death. What you have to be afraid of is your own fears.

Psychological Reflection

Who could be a better expert on fear than Epictetus? Living as a slave in Rome in those times meant that any day could have been your last. Your destiny was uncertain and realistically, you couldn't expect much from life. It meant obeying orders, enduring injustice, pain and hunger. Your life was worth nothing.

When a person who has had a life like this tells us that we don't have to be afraid, why should we fear the far less serious things that happen in our lives?

Quite regularly, what we fear does not even come to pass. Our fears hold us back from trying, being happy and living life to the fullest. It's often by facing our fears that we begin to regain a sense of control over our lives.

23

WHAT DO YOU HOLD ON TO?

Question/comment from a seeker:

When I look at the people in power, I wonder when a catastrophe will happen—whether it is economic, environmental or a tragedy concerning our health. We cannot feel safe if we have rulers and bosses who do not look after our well-being.

Epictetus' answer (*Maxims*, Of Religion and Gods, 17):

Is it not strange that to feel secure, you need a certain kind of government in your country or a certain person in charge of your work? Do you not feel that God's protection is enough to keep you safe when He is our true protector and father?

Psychological Reflection

Many of us live with a false sense of security. We believe that just because we have a job with a permanent contract in a stable organisation, we already have a 'secure' career. We get married, have children and believe that we have a 'secure' life as a couple. Or we get citizenship in a 'secure' country and think that our life is 'secured'.

But according to the Stoics, it is absurd to cling to external things, which are changeable and beyond our control. Epictetus suggests relying on God, the real nurturing 'boss', to take life more calmly and philosophically.

How do you think your faith influences your psychology, emotions and sensitivity? How do you take care of your spiritual needs?

24

THE THREE STEPS OF LEARNING

Question/comment from a seeker:

What is the best way to learn something? I have read many books on personal development, but I don't think I learnt much.

Epictetus' answer (*The Enchiridion*, Chapter XLIX):

I want to understand and accept life and nature as it is. So, I look for a book that can help me, but it turns out that this is not enough—I need someone to explain it to me. I look for an interpreter, someone who has put the theory into practice. And then, finally, the most important and virtuous task awaits me: practising in my daily life what I have learnt.

Psychological Reflection

Epictetus reminds us that true learning consists of three steps.

First, we must have the will to learn, to want to understand life and our nature. The second step is to look for what or who can teach us. And the third and most important step is to put what we have learnt into practice.

Remember the last time you wanted to learn something? Maybe it was playing an instrument, acquiring the skills to fix something broken, or training in a new sport, etc. What steps did you follow? Do they resemble what Epictetus advises us to adhere to?

Now think of a current concern you need to find a solution to. How would you apply Epictetus' three steps to solve it?

25

HOW TO TRAIN YOUR VIRTUES

Question/comment from a seeker:

There are many toxic people around me. What can I do so that I am not so affected when dealing with them?

Epictetus' answer (*Maxims*, Of True Philosophy, 1):

If you tell me that I have a bad father or a bad neighbour, I will tell you that they are mostly bad for themselves, but not for me. To me, they serve as opportunity to practise my gentleness, my generosity and my patience.

Psychological Reflection

If you want to be a dog trainer, and you only get good and easy dogs to practise with, you won't learn much. The day you get a difficult one, you won't know how to handle it. And so it is with many other things in life.

With this reflection, Epictetus encourages us to keep a positive attitude and see 'the good in the bad'. He tells us that by dealing with difficult people, he can practise his virtues, and this, in turn, benefits him.

Think of a toxic person you deal with frequently and ask yourself: what virtue can I practise thanks to him or her? Why has life placed this person in my way? What can I learn?

26

PEOPLE ARE CONTAGIOUS

Question/comment from a seeker:

Should I help others see their mistakes and put them back on the right track?

Epictetus' answer (*Maxims*, Of Self-improvement, 69):

The people you associate with play an important role in your life. Do not hang out with people with no values under the impression that you will change them. Unless you have perfect self-control, it is more likely that they will be a negative influence on you. So, deal with problematic people with great care and wisdom.

Psychological Reflection

People's mental state is contagious, just like their emotions, lifestyles, habits, etc. We often think that we are going to get someone to change thanks to our company, but that is not what usually happens.

Epictetus does not recommend frequenting people who can be a bad influence. He expects us to be very discerning when it comes to those with whom we associate. We should ask ourselves: is this person a good influence? If I had a child, would I want them to be his or her role model? Would people who love me and want the best for me like this person? What sort of mental and emotional state am I in after meeting this person?

Our mental health depends a lot on how well we select the people we get close to.

27

YOUR DESIRES

Question/comment from a seeker:

I am depressed because I will never be able to fulfil all my wishes.

Epictetus' answer (*The Enchiridion*, Chapter II):

As for wishes, it is better to forget about them. For if you desire things that do not depend on you, you will feel anxious. And if you are trying to fulfil desires that are both dependent on you and are virtuous, they may not yet be within your reach and you will have to keep working on them.

Psychological Reflection

Desires are like Hercules' Hydra: we cut off one head (we satisfy one desire) and three more pop up in its place. But how many of these desires are dependent on us and attainable?

Nowadays, most young people want to be millionaires, have a perfect body, a mansion and a collection of luxury cars. But when they go home on the bus after a hard day's work that earns them a thousand dollars a month, open their mobile phones and look at their social networks, what happens? They become frustrated, anxious and depressed as they compare themselves with billionaires and with lives they may never have.

Epictetus proposes that if we have desires, it is better that they are in our control, that they help us become better and more humble people.

In the end, Hercules had to burn the heads of the Hydra (the endless earthly desires) with fire (inner light and wisdom) so that they would not grow back and attack him.

28

WHY DO WE MAKE MISTAKES?

Question/comment from a seeker:

I have been wrong so many times in love that I no longer know what I am really looking for, or what a 'good partner' is.

Epictetus' answer (*Maxims*, Of Self-knowledge, 3):

We all know deep down what is right and wrong, what is just and unjust, about happiness and misfortune. We know how to be responsible and what the problems of being irresponsible are.

How is it then possible that we make so many mistakes? Because we are biased, unreasonable and don't always use our common sense.

Psychological Reflection

Making mistakes is human, life is a learning process. But what happens if we make mistakes over and over again in the same situation without reflecting on it?

What things do you get wrong frequently, as if you can't get out of the loop? Sometimes we seem to follow a script when it comes to love, friendship or work, where we always end up in the wrong. If so, we can ask ourselves: what can I do differently so that I don't get it wrong again next time? What signals am I ignoring, what mistake am I making in the learning process?

For example, in love, if you always choose unsuitable partners, what signals will you have to stay alert for the next time you meet someone? What can you look out for and what do you have to make clear on your part from the beginning to get out of this repetitive script?

Epictetus recommends thinking well before acting, and following our values so that we do not get carried away by our emotional autopilot and prejudices. This will make it easier to choose well and be happy.

29

EXCESSIVE WORRY

Question/comment from a seeker:

What if my partner stops loving me? What if my boss thinks I'm a bad worker? What if I end up in trouble in the future? What if ...?

Epictetus' answer (*Maxims*, Of Self-knowledge, 5):

You are blind and unfair to yourself! You could choose to focus only on what is up to you, but instead, you worry about a thousand things that you cannot control and that keep you from enjoying a good life.

Psychological Reflection

Do you cause yourself unnecessary suffering?

The philosopher recommends refocusing your attention to worry less, giving more importance to what you can manage and accepting everything else as inevitable.

For the Stoics, worrying about how others see us or fretting about tomorrow's losses is as absurd as blaming the rain for making us wet. If it rains, we can use an umbrella to protect ourselves; this is in our own hands.

How can you better protect yourself from worrying about things that are not in your power?

30

ACT WITH HUMILITY AND HUMOUR

Question/comment from a seeker:

I am sensitive to criticism, and I find it upsetting when people speak ill of me behind my back. What can I do about this?

Epictetus' answer (*The Enchiridion*, Chapter XXXIII):

If you become aware that someone is criticising you behind your back, don't defend yourself against what they have said. Instead, reply, 'Well, it seems that they don't know me well enough; if they did, they would have spoken about my other faults too.'

Psychological Reflection

Stoic response to criticism: humility and humour.

In psychology, some exercises propose the use of humour with exaggeration as a technique to deflect when someone criticises us. According to this method, if someone tells you, for example, 'You have put on some weight!' you would say something like, 'Yes, I know! People actually congratulate me because they think I'm pregnant.'

They say that Socrates was capable of laughing at himself. He was mimicked during a theatre performance with a full house, and Socrates stood up and gestured to indicate that it was him they were making fun of, showing that he was not bothered by the mockery.

Think about a recent criticism you have received—how can you exaggerate it with humour to get a good laugh, instead of becoming annoyed?

31

HOLD ON OR LET GO

Question/comment from a seeker:

The lifestyle I wish to lead is beyond my means, but I refuse to accept it. What do you recommend?

Epictetus' answer (*Maxims*, Of Self-improvement, 17):

A child reached into a jar of sweets with a narrow opening and tried to take so many that he was unable to pull his fist out. He had to tearfully let go of almost all his bounty to free himself.

You are this child: you desire too much, and you cannot have it all. Desire less, reduce your excessive ambition, and you will see your wishes satisfied.

Psychological Reflection

All of us are this child at some point in life. We realise that we can't have it all. Sometimes, we have to make a choice and go without the prize we wanted so much. Material desires often trap us and we end up having to choose between owning something and enslaving ourselves, or giving up on our wants and looking for the things in life that can help us gain our freedom.

Personal satisfaction depends on selecting our desires wisely and having mental flexibility. If we choose an achievable and ethical desire and are willing to compromise on our expectations, it will be easier to find contentment.

Some desires enslave us. The irony is that this often happens before we attain what we yearn for—because of the impatient waiting it entails and the anxiety that comes with wanting something—and we are unable to escape even after our wants are fulfilled (if I desire a big house with a garden and a swimming pool, I am now 'enslaved' due to all the work that comes with maintaining the property and upholding my lifestyle).

Sometimes, it is necessary to let go to free yourself, like in Epictetus' example of the child wishing for sweets.

32

BE A GOOD EXAMPLE

Question/comment from a seeker:

Is it good to share my life philosophy with others? If I am successful in something, should I encourage others to do the same?

Epictetus' answer (*The Enchiridion*, Chapter XLVI):

Don't brag about your philosophy of life, and don't talk to insensitive or ignorant people about your moral principles. Rather, stay faithful to those values. For instance, at a banquet, don't tell others how to eat—eat properly as you should and set a good example.

Psychological Reflection

There is a proverb that goes, 'Words are dwarfs and deeds are giants.'

People will remember you more by how you make them feel and the example you set than by anything you say to them. Being a good person will help you in all your interactions.

Do you use your human values as strengths to solve problems and concerns?

Do you maintain humility, patience and trust in your relationships?

Do you consider yourself a good role model for other people, and why?

33

WHAT ARE YOU WILLING TO DO?

Question/comment from a seeker:

They say that meditation helps you find inner space and freedom, but I can't last more than ten minutes with my eyes closed. What is your opinion on this matter?

Epictetus' answer (*Maxims*, Of Liberty and Slavery, 9):

Many people expose themselves to great danger in search of a 'false freedom': they venture into the sea and jump from towering heights; whole cities end up in flames ... And yet, you do not expect to have to give your time and attention, nor make even a small sacrifice for the sake of true freedom?

Psychological Reflection

Epictetus speaks to us on many occasions about the price of every achievement in our lives. If we want to attain inner freedom, learn to manage emotions or handle our obsessions better, we must invest our time and dedication.

How many authoritative books on worry management have you seriously studied?

How long have you attended psychotherapy sessions?

How many years of meditation and relaxation exercises have you gone through?

Have you decided to dedicate yourself to your personal growth as if it were something that will last a lifetime?

As Epictetus says, what do you expect to achieve if you are not willing to make any sacrifices?

34

HOW TO SUCCEED IN LIFE

Question/comment from a seeker:

How can I be successful in life?

Epictetus' answer (*The Enchiridion*, Chapter XIII):

You will always be invincible if you never engage in a struggle where victory does not depend on you.

Psychological Reflection

What does success mean to you? We all know what the word means, but do we really stop to think about what specific tasks need be accomplished so we can consider ourselves successful?

For some people, it means being good at what you do; for others, it entails being the best. There is a big difference between the two concepts—while one can easily make you feel successful, the other may never give you satisfaction because you will always find someone who is 'better'. For some people, being successful means having money, but how much is enough?

What if we think of success as being able to resolve our problems? Most of us can feel successful if we think this way.

Epictetus recommends that we focus only on those things that depend on us and are, hence, achievable.

Reflect for a moment on what success means to you and then think about whether it fits Epictetus' guideline: is it hundred per cent dependent on you, and achievable?

35

SOLITUDE DOES NOT EXIST

Question/comment from a seeker:

I'm scared of being alone.

Epictetus' answer (*Maxims*, Of Religion and the Gods, 7):

When night falls and you are in your room with the door closed, do not think that you are alone. No matter where you are, even if your surroundings seem deserted, never think that you are isolated; you are not.

Psychological Reflection

There is an Indian story that goes like this: to test his potential disciples, a master asks a couple of them to kill a chicken 'where no one can see it'.

One disciple goes into a room, closes the door, kills the chicken and brings the carcass to the master. The second one brings the chicken back alive and says, 'I locked myself in a room, and I was going to kill the chicken, but I remembered that my master said, "where no one can see it". No matter where, the chicken can see me, I can see the chicken, and God can see both the chicken and me. So, it will never be possible to kill the chicken where no one can see it.'

The master accepted this second man; he was the true disciple.

Regardless of whether you believe in God, are an agnostic or a sceptic, doesn't your conscience go with you everywhere? For the Stoic, there is no such thing as solitude.

How would it improve your life to know that solitude does not exist? Why?

36

YOU CHOOSE THE BOAT, NOT THE STORM

Question/comment from a seeker:

I'm not good at making choices. I tend to choose careers that later bore me, I buy things I end up not using and I can't even choose a partner. What can I do?

Epictetus' answer (*Maxims*, Of Resigning, 5):

We should always focus on the things that depend on us, while remaining steadfast and calm about everything else. If I am forced to travel on a ship, what should I do? Well, all that is in my power and seems reasonable to me is: choose the ship, the port and the day of the voyage, and be informed about the captain and crew. But if we run into a storm on the high seas, what happens is no longer up to me.

Psychological Reflection

When you are looking for a new job, a new house or even a new partner, take a moment and reflect first on the characteristics you are looking for. What criteria should it meet? And considering that list, ask yourself the following question: what depends on me and what doesn't?

Let's look at the example of the job. Think about all the expectations you have about a job. You consider the working hours, the salary and the distance between your home and workplace, and you choose a job based on this. So now you've thought about the things that are most important to you when it comes to employment and you've found a job that meets those requirements.

But then you come across colleagues who are not nice or tasks that you didn't know were part of your job description. Does this mean you made the wrong choice? No, because those things were out of your control; you couldn't choose them.

Now it is up to you to figure out what you can do to resolve the problems at your current job, and be at peace with those things that you cannot change.

37

THE ATTITUDE OF A SICK PERSON

Question/comment from a seeker:

Why is it so hard for us to recognise and improve our weaknesses?

Epictetus' answer (*Maxims*, Of Philosophy and Philosophers, 18):

A doctor treats a sick man and tells him, 'Since you have a fever, drink a lot of water.' The sick person obeys the advice without complaining, pays the doctor and is grateful.

On the other hand, when a philosopher or a wise person tells an ignorant person, 'You are too driven by your desires, you suffer from irrational fears and you have false beliefs about quite a few things,' they get angry and offended.

What is the reason for this difference in attitude? It is simple. The sick person feels their illness while the ignorant person does not.

Psychological Reflection

Socrates said that true wisdom comes from recognising one's ignorance. Epictetus, an admirer of Socrates, says something similar when he compares the sick person to the ignorant. The sick person knows that something is wrong with them and trusts the health expert to make them better. The ignorant person is not aware of what is wrong with them and therefore, does not accept any guidelines or advice.

And you, have you ever rejected good advice that was directed at your character? How do you react when someone points out a weakness of yours in a constructive way, in the spirit of helping? Do you think your attitude is more like that of a sick person seeking help or that of an ignorant person?

38

TRUST AND CAUTION

Question/comment from a seeker:

I don't know whether it is better to try and control everything to ensure that things go well, or ignore everything and refrain from intervening, trusting that everything will be alright.

Epictetus' answer (*Maxims*, Of the Deceptive Opinion of Things, 15):

Just because you are careful about what you think or do—both about others and your life—does not mean that you are distrustful. It is up to you to find the right balance between caution and trust. Your best option is to be careful about the things that depend on you and confident about those things that are not completely in your control.

Psychological Reflection

Trust in things that do not depend on us and be cautious about that which does. If we acted according to this maxim of Epictetus, we would certainly suffer less. Let us imagine two scenarios:

In a job interview, we would act with caution and intelligence, because what we say and do in that occasion completely depends on us. Afterwards, we would be relaxed and calm, because we know that the outcome (whether we are hired or not) is not up to us.

When we educate a child, many things are in our hands—the values we pass on, the example we set for the child, etc. When they become an adult and are able to make their own decisions, we would trust that things will go well for them. We would no longer hover over their shoulder, control their lifestyle or try to make decisions for them.

Think about an issue that worries you, and analyse the part that depends on you (treat it with caution) and the part that does not (treat it with trust). How does your degree of concern change?

39

EVERYTHING HAS ITS PRICE

Question/comment from a seeker:

I often compare myself to people who have more money, more possessions or more fame than I do, and I can't help thinking that they are probably happier than I am.

Epictetus' answer (*The Enchiridion*, Chapter XXV):

What is the price of lettuce? Let's say it is one dollar. If someone pays a dollar, they get a head of lettuce. Now imagine that you have determined not to spend on lettuce, and so you don't get it. But don't think that you have less than the person who bought it. Just as that person has the lettuce, so you have the dollar that you did not spend.

Psychological Reflection

With this metaphor, Epictetus invites us to reflect on the fact that everything has its price. You may see someone in possession of something that you would like to have and be overcome with feelings of envy, sadness or anger. But you are not taking into account what it cost the person to get that house, car, holiday or whatever it is you envy. You don't know the sacrifices he or she had to make to obtain all they have now—maybe they worked overtime, maybe they had to spend all their savings, maybe they had to fight with their partner, or take up another job and go without free time ...

The next time you compare yourself and feel you have less than another person, remember that everything has its price and that you might not be prepared to pay the real or emotional price that the other person was willing to pay.

40

DON'T LIMIT YOURSELF

Question/comment from a seeker:

I am too much of a 'nice person'. I don't like to draw attention to myself and I tend to adapt to others, but then later I regret it.

Epictetus' answer (*Maxims*, Of Self-improvement, 72):

Don't be limited by your friends and don't stop making positive changes in your life for fear of being laughed at.

What do you prefer: to be someone with no values who is liked by unpleasant people, or do what you think is right at the risk of being criticised?

Psychological Reflection

It is certainly easier to think and act as most people do, especially those we often deal with. It keeps us from looking bad or having to explain ourselves. But can we really say that this is an honest way of living?

Imagine if Gandhi hadn't pursued the cause of non-violence lest he stand out negatively; or if Marie Curie had thought it more appropriate for a woman to stay out of masculine fields like physics and chemistry.

Remember though, that we do not have to contribute anything extraordinary to humanity to follow Epictetus' advice and live an authentic life. Stoics encourage us to always think and do what we believe is right and ethical, regardless of how other people see it. They seek a virtuous life.

Have you ever done something contrary to what the majority of people do because you thought it was the right move? How did it make you feel? What would you say to a friend who is too afraid of societal judgement to stand up for a good cause they believe in?

41

MAKE GOOD USE OF YOUR IMAGINATION

Question/comment from a seeker:

Sometimes, I spend hours thinking about possible dangers in the future and I still don't come up with a satisfactory solution. What can I think or do in these situations?

Epictetus' answer (*The Enchiridion*, Chapter I):

When you imagine unpleasant things and get emotionally affected, you can speak to that contrived fantasy and say, 'You are just a figment of my imagination, you are not real.' Then analyse whether the scenarios you are thinking up would actually be within your control (if or when they actualise). If you conclude that it is beyond your control, you can move on saying 'this is not my problem'.

Psychological Reflection

When do we feel most anxious? When we anticipate a catastrophic future and obsess about possible threats, when our minds reach for what our life is not yet ready to receive, and when we believe that we don't have enough resources. Most of the anxiety we experience stems from us using our imagination wrong.

But it is up to us whether we use our imagination to our advantage or disadvantage. Many people use it to solve problems, be creative in their work, be happier in relationships and achieve a better quality of life.

Epictetus suggests that we differentiate imagination from reality in order to suffer less. Often, the reality is richer and more nuanced than fiction. There may be plenty of resources, personal strengths and support available to us in real life that goes unnoticed when we are anxious about the future.

A well-known quote goes: if you can't control it, why worry about it, and if you can control it, why worry about it?

If you find that it is not up to you to take control of this train, just relax and enjoy the ride.

42

DON'T TRY TO AVOID THE INEVITABLE

Question/comment from a seeker:

I panic about ending up poor, getting sick or dying, and I always end up doing a thousand things to stay away from this future.

Epictetus' answer (*The Enchiridion*, Chapter II):

If you spend your life trying to avoid sickness, death or poverty, you will be a miserable person.

Psychological Reflection

According to Epictetus, to live trying to avoid unpleasant things at all times is to be a slave, a prisoner of fear. This is not to say that fear is not useful and intuitive at times. The problem comes when it is excessive and when it paralyses and blocks us unnecessarily, taking us away from the kind of person we want to become.

The Buddha discovered at a very young age that sickness, old age and death are inevitable. So, instead of avoiding them or pretending they did not exist, he spent the rest of his life seeking inner freedom. He could not control the external factors that could affect us all, but after many years of searching, he conquered his inner world, and in doing so, became enlightened.

The Buddha and Epictetus have shared many views on what makes us suffer and what liberates us—our state of mind, what we avoid and what we seek in life.

43

HUMAN VALUES

Question/comment from a seeker:

What do you think of selfish people?

Epictetus' answer (*Maxims*, Of Friendship, 3):

A life dominated by 'me' and 'mine' is similar to the life of an animal. It does not suit an intelligent being that can use reason. If the 'me', that is, my interests, are aligned with values such as honesty, justice, and so forth, then I will be a good friend, a good child, a good parent and a good spouse; but if I only think of my interests, I will no longer be good.

Psychological Reflection

Here, we are told that a life based on our ego brings us nothing good. How can we live better? According to Epictetus, a good way to break free from the chains of 'me' and 'mine' is to live adhering to human values.

Think of a problem in your life today—what virtue do you need to feel better about the issue: generosity, honesty, perseverance, friendship, hope, patience, serenity, trust? What can you do on your part to nurture the value you need?

The Dalai Lama once said that it is very difficult to be happy without human values. It seems that Epictetus would have agreed.

44

THE BODY IS ONLY ONE PART OF YOU

Question/comment from a seeker:

How can I feel good if I am ill or suffering from chronic pain?

Epictetus' answer (*The Enchiridion*, Chapter IX):

Illness limits the body, not the will. A limp limits your legs, but not your determination. Repeat this to yourself whenever something happens to your body, and you will realise that while it limits a part of you, it cannot restrain your essence, your soul.

Psychological Reflection

When a person can no longer do something due to illness, they may go through the stages of grief.

First, they refuse to accept their new limitation and try to find alternative solutions to their problem. When they realise that this is unrealistic, feelings of anger, grief and sadness set in. But after a while, if the person does not get stuck in that stage, they reach acceptance.

Who copes best and the quickest? Those who focus on what they can still do, despite their new limitations. They will adapt better to their reality, have better self-esteem and suffer less.

What can you do today to enjoy life more without depending too much on your current physical condition?

45

THE ROLE YOU HAVE BEEN GIVEN

Question/comment from a seeker:

I tend to think I'm unlucky when compared with others, and this makes me anxious.

Epictetus' answer (*The Enchiridion*, Chapter XVII):

Remember that you are an actor in a 'drama'. The director decides the part you are to play: if he wants your performance to be brief, it will be brief; if he wants it to be long, it will be long. If he wants you to play a beggar, try to play him naturally; the same goes if your role is that of a judge, a king or an ordinary person.

In other words, the only thing you have to do is competently represent the character that has been assigned to you, but it is up to someone else to chooses the role that fits you.

Psychological Reflection

In order to suffer less, we sometimes have to adjust our expectations to reality and recognise our limits. This does not mean that we should refrain from striving to achieve our goals. But we need to understand that there is also destiny. Life is full of twists and turns, and not everything is in our hands. Man proposes, life disposes.

The time and place where you were born, the parents you have, the education you receive and the circumstances in which you live—all of these factors influence your chances of being 'somebody' in society. But none of this was your decision. You can only choose how you perceive it, how you take it, and how you respond to it all. You might have a good hand or a bad hand, but you choose how you play your cards.

How better will your well-being fare when you accept the inevitable things in life? Can you reflect on the life of a wise person in human history and see what they did in the face of their circumstances?

46

THE EMOTIONAL PRICE

Question/comment from a seeker:

There is an important change I want to make in my life, but I am putting it off because I am afraid of the reaction of the people around me.

Epictetus' answer (*The Enchiridion*, Chapter XXII):

If you want to make a change in your life related to your inner development, be prepared for criticism and ridicule from others. They will say things like, 'Now he pretends to be a philosopher!' and 'Now he thinks he's better than everyone else!'

Do what you think is right, but don't think you are better than anyone else. If you remain firm in your personal development, those who once laughed at you will admire you later. But if you are discouraged by them, it will be like losing twice—you will disappoint yourself and others.

Psychological Reflection

Time and again, the Stoics recommend that we make light of people's taunts and criticisms, as we cannot control what others think. But we can still do what we believe is right.

Since it feels good when others approve of what we say or do, this can lead to a certain degree of dependency. Sometimes, we may even choose not to do what we like, delay important changes, or withhold our opinion on certain issues, for fear of disapproval.

Being different requires courage. But it can also inspire others and encourage them to make changes they did not dare make before.

Have you ever dared to be 'different'? How did it make you feel? Do you think it inspired someone else?

47

REAL WEALTH

Question/comment from a seeker:

How can a person who does not have much money be calm and happy?

Epictetus' answer (*Maxims*, Of Richness, 2):

Your present wealth does not depend on you, but your happiness does. Material wealth may be short-lived; it quickly runs out. However, the happiness you gain from wisdom stays with you for the rest of your life.

Psychological Reflection

We seem to be enamoured with the accumulation of material 'toys' that break and get damaged with time. But the wise person's priority is to achieve lasting inner happiness. They are aware that the happiness that comes from worldly possessions have an expiry date, and so they devote time and energy to their inner development.

The happiest children are not those who have the most toys, but those who know how to play with the toys they already have. Children don't want toys; what they want is to play and have fun.

How can self-awareness help you enjoy your life better?

48

KNOW YOUR STRENGTHS

Question/comment from a seeker:

I've chosen a job that I'm not very good at. What can I do now?

Epictetus' answer (*The Enchiridion*, Chapter XXIX):

Examine the task you need to do, and then see if your nature fits the task and if you can handle the load. Do you want to compete in a sport? Examine your arms, legs and muscles, because everyone is born with different strengths.

Psychological Reflection

Sometimes, we get surprised by our strengths! It's important that we recognise our advantages and are aware of them. How would you feel if, due to a car accident, you had to give up your dream of being a football player in your country's national team? What if you then left football behind and started singing and playing the guitar, selling millions of music records? This is the true story of singer Julio Iglesias.

Often, we insist on doing certain tasks without knowing what we are good at, without knowing what we will shine at. You may suffer when, due to circumstances, you are unable to do a certain job, but that doesn't mean that you can't succeed in other areas. Sometimes, we rediscover ourselves along the way and end up surprising our personal expectations.

What are your strengths and in what contexts are they most appreciated?

49

REVIEW YOUR THOUGHTS

Question/comment from a seeker:
Sometimes, I think that I am good for nothing and that I can't expect anything good from life. What can I do when I think bad things about myself?

Epictetus' answer (*Maxims*, Of Self-improvement, 2):

You can see how any banker will carefully examine the money he is given so as not to be cheated. He uses his senses for this: his sight, his touch, etc.

We are all like 'bankers' when it comes to the things that we find interesting: when something motivates us, we pay attention to it with all our senses to make sure we understand it right.

But it seems that the prospect of analysing our thoughts does not motivate us enough, because we usually believe our thoughts as if they were all valid and useful.

Psychological Reflection

We cannot always choose what we think. Many of our thoughts are automatic and are based on our upbringing, culture, emotional state, current situation in life, and so on. You may be reading this now and thinking 'reading this is very boring' or 'this philosopher is very interesting'. But whatever your thoughts are, you have not chosen it, although it is up to you to validate and believe what comes into your mind.

Only you can decide what you do with what you think. You can run your thoughts through a filter and evaluate whether it is useful and practical, or whether it makes you feel good to think that way.

You can practise intentional thinking, repeat constructive ideas to yourself, or read books that help you.

Let's do a little exercise.

How are you feeling right now? What are you thinking about yourself, others and life?

Are you able to see the connection between what you think and what you feel?

What thoughts about yourself do you find useful enough in order to mentally repeat to gain confidence?

50

COPY THE WISE

Question/comment from a seeker:

When I have to talk to a senior colleague at work, I become nervous.

Epictetus' answer (*The Enchiridion*, Chapter XXXIII):

If you have to meet with someone you believe is superior to you in terms of any particular metric, think about what Socrates or Zeno [a Stoic master] would have done in your place. You will find it easier to face whatever might happen in that meeting.

Psychological Reflection

In many situations, it helps to have a role model.

Choose someone who has the skills and wisdom that would be of assistance to you.

Can you imagine that person in detail? Their posture, how they would express themselves, how they would speak—at what speed and how loudly?

Before you meet with someone higher up on the professional ladder, put yourself in the shoes of this wiser and more skilled person you chose as your role model. How do you feel? Does your perception of the situation change? How do you view yourself and others when you are this person? Is there something you realise now what you hadn't before?

51

DO IT ANYWAY

Question/comment from a seeker:

I wish to do something that my family and friends wouldn't approve of. Would it be better to do it in secret and avoid arguments, or should I be open about my actions?

Epictetus' answer (*The Enchiridion*, Chapter XXXV):

If you are convinced that you are doing something good, don't worry about others getting wind of it, even if they wouldn't agree with your actions.

If your behaviour doesn't adhere to human values, avoid acting; but if you are true to your conscience, why should you worry about those who criticise you unfairly?

Psychological Reflection

Many people hide their actions or stop doing good things—going to a psychologist, studying what they really want to, prioritising self-care, etc.—for fear of what others will say.

If you worry about what other people think to the point where you stop doing good things, you will lose your mental focus and become unhappy in the long run.

If what you do is aligned with your values, if it brings you closer to inner calm and happiness, if you know you are acting righteously and not hurting anyone ... why should you continue to worry about others and their opinions?

52

ARE YOU AN OBSTACLE TO YOURSELF?

Question/comment from a seeker:

My whole lifestyle is a contradiction: I care about my health but I don't exercise. I want to switch jobs but I don't send out my CV. I want to pass my exams but I don't study. I love my partner but I don't spend quality time with them. I know what would make me feel good but I don't do it. What advice do you have for me?

Epictetus' answer (*Maxims*, Of Self-improvement, 29):

Agrippinus offers us an inspiring phrase: I will never be an obstacle to myself.

Psychological Reflection

We all have an 'inner saboteur' inside us who sometimes puts off important tasks and makes excuses for the sake of protecting us or avoiding discomfort.

For example, we want to take care of our body, and so we join a gym. And then we have thoughts like, 'I don't have time to train ... It's too expensive to go to the gym ... Will I really be able to get in shape with the belly I have?' And in the end, we end up at home, watching TV and eating pizza. Our internal saboteur 'protects' us from the discomfort of training. Comfort and pleasure win temporarily, but self-esteem worsens in the long-term.

In what situations are you an obstacle to yourself? What feelings (fear, embarrassment, loss of comfort, etc.) are you avoiding when you put off something important for later? What can you do so that you take care of important things in your life while staying in your comfort zone?

53

THE HIDDEN ENEMY

Question/comment from a seeker:

How will I know that I am making progress in my personal development? That I am no longer affected by things in the same way as before, that I am becoming more Stoic?

Epictetus' answer (*The Enchiridion*, Chapter XLVIII):

Signs that a person takes things philosophically: they do not criticise anyone, they do not praise anyone for self-serving reasons, they do not complain about anyone, they do not accuse anyone, and they refrain from self-praise and boastful behaviour.

They do not care if others think they are foolish or ignorant. In short, they remain attentive to their inner self, monitoring their ego as if it were a hidden enemy.

Psychological Reflection

If you were the kind of person Epictetus describes, you would probably be more carefree, calm and happy.

What prevents us from living this way? Our ego—the proud part of us which thinks that we are superior to other people.

But in all mystical, spiritual and philosophical traditions, importance is placed on dissolving the ego and going beyond that false identity to seek true answers to the question, 'Who am I?'

Epictetus encourages us to keep an eye on this 'hidden enemy', sharpen our thinking and remain calm.

54

YOUR FIGHTING SPIRIT

Question/comment from a seeker:

When something goes wrong, I don't feel like trying again. I am discouraged whenever things don't work out for me despite my earnest efforts.

Epictetus' answer (*Maxims*, Of Self-improvement, 73):

Never let anything discourage you. Rather, imitate the masters of combat who force the novice to get up and return to the fight every time they hit the mat. Do the same with your spirit; as long as you are resolute in your efforts, the results will follow.

Psychological Reflection

What governs your fighting spirit? What controls your courage?

Everything you can nurture, grow and develop depends on you. For example, your fighting spirit can be nurtured through mental images, the ideas that you repeat to yourself, what you choose to do, the people and places you frequent, etc.

Remember an experience that has been a source of encouragement for you in the past. It could be an inspiring place you visited, people who have motivated you, or something you experienced that made you feel like life has meaning. To experience that emotional state, you must surely have done something; what was it? Can you repeat what you did back then now in the present to make yourself feel something similar?

Your feelings are not something you can control. But you can still decide what you do with these feelings, how you interpret them and what actions you'll take.

55

FREEDOM IS ALL IN THE MIND

Question/comment from a seeker:

If everyone always did what they wanted, the world would be in chaos. But we would experience more freedom, wouldn't we?

Epictetus' answer (*Maxims*, Of Liberty and Slavery, 22):

When the wise speak of freedom, they do not mean that you should despise authority. No philosopher has ever taught you to rebel against your sovereign or deny them what is their due.

I teach those who are interested in listening to me how to take care of their thoughts. Thoughts are dependent only on the thinker and are totally free, because God decided that we can be the exclusive masters of what we think.

Psychological Reflection

We do not have a say in who assumes a position of leadership, nor can we change the laws of a country. But we can manage our interpretations of what is happening and choose the strategy which will help us deal with what is going on.

Epictetus was a slave who realised how to achieve inner freedom. He learnt to master his mind and knew how to focus on the essential and react in the best manner, given his circumstances.

Is there a situation in your present life where you feel powerless, with little freedom? It could be a family problem, financial issue, work trouble, etc. How does what you think about your situation affect your feelings? Despite your circumstances, what could you think, appreciate or do to attain more freedom and peace?

56

PREFER WHAT GOD CHOOSES

Question/comment from a seeker:

Nothing has been going well in my life lately.

Epictetus' answer (*Maxims*, Of Religion and Gods, 2):

If something happens, it is because God wants it, and I personally prefer that to any of my other wishes. Because I am convinced that God can choose what is good for me better than I can. And I dedicate all my actions, will and fears to him. In short: I want what God wants in my life.

Psychological Reflection

Here is someone who was a slave, telling us that he prefers what God chooses for him.

And we who enjoy many comforts in life and are 'free' enough to be able to make important decisions for ourselves, complain that things are not going well for us.

It is estimated that if you have food in your fridge, some clothes to wear, a roof over your head and a place to sleep, you are richer than most of the world. And if you also have money in the bank, in your purse and some loose change, you are among the world's richest.

Take a moment to think about all the good things that you have in your life. Think also about those things you take for granted and never imagined living without. Then go back to your worry and contrast it with this perspective.

57

TAKE CARE OF YOUR SOUL

Question/comment from a seeker:

I am afraid to die.

Epictetus' answer (*Maxims*, Of Death, 8):

Everyone fears the death of the body. But who cares about the vitality of the soul?

Psychological Reflection

There are people who are afraid of dying because they feel that they have not yet lived. Others fear dying because they do not know what they will experience after death. Some fear suffering at the moment of death and afterwards.

In every case, the Stoic prescription for the fear of death is to take care of one's soul. That is, to try make the best of our life—to be an exemplary human being with good values, taking care of not just our body and mind, but also of our inner human essence.

What would your soul say if it could speak to you and give you an opinion about your life? How could you take better care of the vitality of your soul, as Epictetus suggests?

58

DON'T COMPLAIN ABOUT BEING ALONE

Question/comment from a seeker:

When I'm alone, I go crazy ... in the end, I always end up calling someone or meeting a friend.

Epictetus' answer (*Maxims*, Miscellaneous, 56):

What do children do when they are alone? They entertain themselves by looking for stones or building sand castles, which they then destroy. Children always find a way to entertain and amuse themselves. And what they do out of pure childish grace, can't you do with your will and wisdom? We should never complain about being alone.

Psychological Reflection

Seneca says that you are never alone if you are your own friend. For the Stoics, solitude is an opportunity to learn to be at ease with oneself, and a chance to remember that we are never really alone, because the one who created everything is always by our side.

What is loneliness for you? Do you think it is possible to feel it even if you are in the company of many people, and vice versa?

How does your view of loneliness change when you imagine that you are never alone and that there is a God (or a force or energy) always with you?

59

THINGS COME AND GO

Question/comment from a seeker:

It has taken me a lot of effort and sacrifice to earn a good living. I am afraid of losing my job and my possessions, and having to start from scratch.

Epictetus' answer (*Maxims*, Miscellaneous, 59):

You have nothing that has not been given to you. He who gives you everything can also take it away from you. You are, then, not only foolish but also ungrateful and unfair when you try to go against this truth.

Psychological Reflection

Even if you believe that everything you have earned in your life is through your own merit, according to the Stoics, you should be humble and not forget that it is God who gives and takes away everything. For if what you have is really yours, no one could ever take it away from you.

Epictetus reminds us that everything we possess has been given to us. Of course, there is a part that we control; a part that we have earned with our effort, strategy and time. But it is mentally healthier to accept that as fast as things come, they can also go, and we have less control than we think we do. Once we realise this, we won't have such a hard time when one day, we have to say goodbye to something dear to us.

60

THE PRISONER OF PLEASURE

Question/comment from a seeker:

When I like something, I find it hard to control myself. But I believe that life's pleasures are important for our well-being.

Epictetus' answer (*The Enchiridion*, Chapter XXXIII):

When you are tempted to let yourself be carried away by a desire or pleasure, avoid getting hooked and becoming its prisoner.

First, do nothing and let some time pass. Then imagine in your mind two scenarios: the first, where you enjoy that pleasure, and then regret it and become upset with yourself. The second is where you abstain from pleasure, and then feel happy and see yourself as a person of intelligence and self-control.

It is up to you to decide which person you want to be.

Psychological Reflection

A fly sitting on the mouth of a jar of honey will enjoy its sweet treat. But if it is not careful, it can get caught in the viscous liquid. The mind and pleasures work in a similar way—the mind is always seeking more pleasure and can never get enough. That is why the Stoics warn us to be more careful and austere.

Epictetus shares with us a simple piece of advice: when you feel the desire for pleasure, stop and think about it first. Let some time pass, so as not to be swept away by the anxiety of the moment. Then do a little mental exercise: imagine having enjoyed that pleasure and regretting it afterwards. And also imagine not having enjoyed the pleasure and feeling proud of yourself.

61

WHEN THE PARTY IS OVER

Question/comment from a seeker:

For people who have money and power, life is easier. I think I would be happier if I had a privileged life.

Epictetus' answer (*Maxims*, Of Liberty and Slavery, 13):

To judge whether a person is free, don't look at his or her social status and power, for those with the highest positions are often the most enslaved.

But you say, 'I see many who do as they please.' Even if this is true, I assure you that these people are slaves who enjoy certain privileges for a limited time, until their 'party' ends. You ask when their party will end? When one day the circumstances of life take those privileges away from them.

Psychological Reflection

It is easy to be fooled by appearances when we see a person with social currency or purchasing power, who seems to be a successful and happy person, completely in control of their own life. Who hasn't compared themselves to such a person? In the age of social media, it is even easier to find out about the lives of others and fall into comparisons.

However, Epictetus warns us that such people are not freer, but the opposite. For they depend on those things, whether power or money, to keep them happy. In other words, they depend on something that fate can take away from them at any moment. And that is what, according to Epictetus, will happen one day: the time will come when their 'party is over' and you will realise how reliant their happiness was on external factors.

If the source of your peace and security is not in your inner self, then you do not yet know the freedom Epictetus speaks of.

62

PEOPLE WHO ARE LOST

Question/comment from a seeker:

I have a hard time dealing with those without morals—selfish people, people who think only about how to get their own way, or those who cheat others.

Epictetus' answer (*Maxims*, Of True Philosophy, 4):

You empathise with a blind or lame person, but can't empathise with a bad person? Evil people are harmed by their own ignorance in spite of themselves, just as a blind person cannot help their lack of sight or a lame person cannot avoid limping.

Psychological Reflection

Marcus Aurelius expressed in *Meditations* that sometimes, we should feel compassion for those people who have lost their way in life. For they are like a blind person who cannot distinguish black from white—their ignorance prevents them from discriminating between good and evil.

Epictetus offers a very similar idea here, stating that we should exercise patience and empathy with those who have strayed from the right path.

How would your view of these people change if, instead of seeing them as evil or selfish, you saw them as lost human beings who have yet to learn much about leading a conscious way of life? Would such a point of view cause you the same pain and anger, or does it change anything in the way you perceive these people?

63

HOW DO YOU RESPOND TO CRITICISM?

Question/comment from a seeker:

How do I stop myself from getting angry with people who treat me badly, criticise me or don't respect me?

Epictetus' answer (*The Enchiridion*, Chapter I):

Don't confuse yourself into thinking that you can control things that are beyond your power; otherwise, you will end up bitter, full of anxiety and prone to arguing with everyone.

But if you focus on what is within your control and accept that there are things that are not in your hands, you will be much better off—you will no longer feel threatened by other people, you will not be pressed into doing things you don't want to, and you will not be so afraid of being hurt.

Psychological Reflection

People will not always agree with us, and may criticise, despise or insult us. This is out of our control, and sometimes unavoidable.

How can we feel better about other people's critical opinions? We can focus on how we respond to these opinions (ignore them, refute them, joke about them, avoid such people, seek support, etc.).

And how can we fortify our mind so that criticism does not affect us too much? We can think in a kinder and gentler way about ourselves. For instance, you can tell yourself, 'I am capable of achieving good things in life. I do my best all the time.'

We can also remember personal achievements from the past that demonstrate our intelligence and strengths when it comes to adapting to life (e.g., I got through school, passed exams, worked in that company, recovered well from that break-up, made those friends, etc.).

64

APPRECIATE WHAT LIFE LENDS YOU

Question/comment from a seeker:

Life is very cruel. How can you feel at peace if you get fired from your job, lose your home or if a loved one dies?

Epictetus' answer (*The Enchiridion*, Chapter XI):

When you lose something, don't think that it has been forcefully taken away from you, but that you have willingly given it back. Has your child died? They have been returned. Have you lost your wife? She has been returned. Has your house been burgled? Those things too, have been returned. You will think, 'But the thief is evil for stealing from me.' The one (God or a higher power) who gave it to you has taken it back. It does not matter how it happened.

While you are permitted to enjoy something or someone, treat it all as if it did not belong to you, just as travellers who pass through a hostel treat the facilities and supplies provided to them.

Psychological Reflection

The mind is designed to look for attachments. This happens to such an extent that, like chewing gum, our mind fastens itself to people, things or even to the past, and becomes so consumed that it suffers unnecessarily.

Personal losses often produce a lot of pain; this is inevitable. What Epictetus suggests is that we refrain from adding fuel to the fire by drawing destructive conclusions. The story we tell ourselves about why we lose something or someone makes a great difference in terms of suffering.

Epictetus repeatedly speaks of his faith in God, the one who grants us all the goods and gifts of life, and even the relationships we have. But he knows that experiences and people come and go with the passage of time. Let us cherish it while it lasts and remember that there is a time to receive and enjoy, and a time to let go. There are many things we cannot change but we can take some measure of comfort in remembering that we have given back to ... (God, life, the universe, etc.).

Despite the losses we face, life goes on and it has meaning.

65

TO APPEAR DOES NOT MEAN TO BE

Question/comment from a seeker:

Sometimes I feel envious when I look at other people's lives. It seems that people who have achieved success in their work, acquired wealth, or found love are happier than I am.

Epictetus' answer (*The Enchiridion*, Chapter XIX):

Don't fool yourself into thinking that someone is happier than you just because they are very powerful, rich or highly valued in society.

Psychological Reflection

Does having millions of followers on social media or millions of dollars in your bank account guarantee that you will have more peace of mind and happiness?

As the Dalai Lama once said, peace of mind, wisdom and happiness have to be created by yourself; these are not things that come from the outside world.

Appearances can be deceiving. Looking happy on social media does not mean you are happy. Mental maturity, human values and psychological resources guarantee more happiness and serenity than scores of followers or all the money in the world.

What motivates you in life? What do you love? What steps do you take to be a happier person?

66

YOU ARE NOT YOUR THOUGHTS

Question/comment from a seeker:
I have hit the wall so many times that I no longer have the motivation to try new things or make positive changes. I might as well accept that I am a loser.

Epictetus' answer (*The Enchiridion*, Chapter XXIV):

When thoughts like, 'I'm going to be miserable all my life' and 'I'll never amount to anything no matter what I do' crosses your mind, don't believe them. You can only excel in something that really depends on you, and that 'something' is where it will be easiest for you to add value.

Psychological Reflection

Nobody likes to fail. But sooner or later, we all lose at something. Why punish ourselves with thoughts like, 'I'm useless … I'm not good at anything … I don't like the way I am', if we can be reasonable, kind and loving to ourselves instead? We can repeat other thoughts like, 'Not everything depends on me, but I'm worthy anyway. I can achieve many good things in my life,' etc.

How do you think you will feel if you make an effort to have a kinder inner dialogue?

And how does what you say to yourself affect the way you treat others and the appreciation you receive from them?

There is a saying about self-esteem: when I love myself more, the world loves me more, and I love the world more.

67

INSULTS

Question/comment from a seeker:

I think it's inevitable that you will feel terrible when you are insulted.

Epictetus' answer (*The Enchiridion*, Chapter XXVIII):

If someone were to offer your person to some random passer-by, it would infuriate you. It is the same with our mind. When people succeed in upsetting you and you are offended by their words, you are offering up your mind to the perpetrator.

Psychological Reflection

It is impossible to please everyone. But we can choose how we respond to the criticism and insults, and what to do when we feel upset.

When we focus on what is up to us and downplay destructive criticism, we will be better at responding to others, and remain calmer.

How do you feel about yourself when you are insulted? Do you believe the insult or do you filter it out?

What affirmations can you think to yourself to protect your inner peace?

How can you better manage your emotions the next time you are criticised? What works best for you?

68

IT ALL DEPENDS ON THE POINT OF VIEW

Question/comment from a seeker:

Today, a person treated me badly for no reason. I thought about this all day long and couldn't get it out of my mind. What can I do if this happens to me again?

Epictetus' answer (*The Enchiridion*, Chapter XLII):

When someone misbehaves towards you through their words or deeds, it is because, from their point of view, they think they have the right to do so. Due to their incorrect perspective, the person is deluding themselves, and will suffer the consequences of their mistake.

Knowing this, don't stress about the person who treats you inappropriately. You can say to yourself: they are acting according to their (incorrect) point of view.

Psychological Reflection

An office worker is yelled at by his boss. Then he comes home angry and yells at his wife. The wife then yells at her son. The son hits the dog. What was the fault of the dog, the son, the wife and the worker?

Are we victims of victims? Sometimes, a whole chain of abuse is generated when we don't set healthy boundaries in time, and we mistreat each other, like a virus that spreads.

Think back to a time when you were treated badly for something that had nothing to do with you. How did you identify that the abuse was unrelated to what you said or did?

Now, try to remember a time when you were the one who treated other people unfairly, because of a bad day you had or because of anger that you had not processed well.

When we know that a person's reaction is inappropriate, it is best not to take it too seriously. Set healthy limits to what you are willing to tolerate so that we don't become part of the chain of irritable, contagious people.

69

CLEAR YOUR MIND

Question/comment from a seeker:

I don't know what is most important to me in life. I'm quite lost and that makes me very anxious and depressed. I think I need to put myself in expert hands.

Epictetus' answer (*Maxims*, Miscellaneous, 29):

If your logical reasoning, which brings order to all that you do, is messed up, who can put it in order other than you?

Psychological Reflection

At therapy, we often meet people who place the responsibility for their mental health on the psychotherapist. But the psychotherapist is merely a companion on our personal journey, sharing with us tools to help ourselves.

Epictetus reminds us that there is no one who knows us better than ourselves, and only we can set our own minds in order. A psychologist can guide us and help us feel less lost, but they cannot fix our lives.

You can ask yourself: what can I do today to feel a little better? What can I do to get more clarity about my life and priorities? Start with small and simple things—every step counts.

70

YOUR WAY OF SEEING THE WORLD

Question/comment from a seeker:

Life is unfair to me. How can I deal with my frustrations more philosophically?

Epictetus' answer (*The Enchiridion*, Chapter XLVIII):

What is the attitude and behaviour of someone who does not aspire to wisdom? They think that both what benefits them and harms them comes from the outside world.

What is the attitude and manner of a wise person? They think that both what benefits them and harms them depends on themselves.

Psychological Reflection

The way we see the world is an indicator of who we are. We may see the world as unjust, think that people are evil and that our existence is futile. If we think this way, how can we expect to feel good about life's challenges?

But we can also think that there is a bit of everything in this life—justice and injustice, both good and evil people—and we have the right to exist, without having to prove anything to anyone in order to feel valuable. How would it change the way we live if we see things this way?

Any problem can be seen as a life challenge: an opportunity to see if we will be able to respond wisely in all circumstances.

How do you think the way you see problems influences the way you deal with them?

71

HOW TO BE OKAY WITH OTHERS

Question/comment from a seeker:

I'm concerned about getting along with people. What advice would you have me follow?

Epictetus' answer (*The Enchiridion*, Chapter XXXIII):

Don't criticise people, don't praise them to get something from them, and don't compare them either.

Psychological Reflection

When we interact with others out of self-interest or fear, we lose their trust and our own objectivity. And when we compare people there is always someone who 'loses' (in comparison to another).

Think of someone you often criticise. Can you identify three good things in that person?

Think of a person you admire. Can you see three things that the person should improve upon?

Now think about the comparisons you usually make. Who do you compare yourself to most often? How does it make you feel?

Is this comparison constructive or destructive for your self-esteem?

72

THERE IS A TIME FOR EVERYTHING

Question/comment from a seeker:

I have already read books on personal development and practised a few exercises, but it takes me a lot of effort to change the way I am or improve in something.

Epictetus' answer (*Maxims*, Miscellaneous, 42):

Nothing of value can be obtained overnight, not even an apple. If you ask me to give you an apple right now, I will tell you to wait for the seed to be sown, the tree to grow and the fruit to ripen. You have to give it time.

And if this is what happens with an apple, how can you expect your spirit to change or improve overnight?

Psychological Reflection

There is a time for everything. Any task at work or at home takes time to complete. We line up to buy things, wait until the bus arrives when we need to travel and we stand by impatiently until the software is installed on our laptop. We are used to waiting and having a little patience for the most normal things in our daily lives.

And if even a household chore takes a while, or, as Epictetus said, an apple requires time to grow, how can we expect to experience immediate changes within us?

The Stoics tell us that the most important task required of us is the work we need to do on ourselves, and it is not a piece of cake. It is a lifetime's work, and yet it is worthwhile. The day to start it is now, and it doesn't matter how much progress we make; it matters that we do it. As Lao Tzu said, a journey of a thousand miles begins with a single step.

73

EVERYTHING HAS A BRIGHT SIDE

Question/comment from a seeker:

What kind of thoughts can I keep in mind to help me through dark times in life?

Epictetus' answer (*The Enchiridion*, Chapter XVIII):

Everything that happens in my life is good for me, as long as I choose it to be. It is up to me to focus on how a situation could be of personal benefit.

Psychological Reflection

My partner has left me? I can learn to enjoy solitude and get to know myself better, meet other interesting people, go on a solo trip, learn something new in my free time, meet my family and friends more often, etc.

I am fired from my workplace? I no longer have to deal with the unpleasant people at work, I can sit back and relax for a while, reinvent myself and try for a better job, etc.

I have health problems? I can use this opportunity to learn to appreciate things I didn't value before, tend to my spiritual needs, cultivate my inner strength and purpose while living with my illness, share my experience with those who suffer from the same condition and connect with new people.

And you, what will you do today to focus on the positive side of what is happening to you?

74

IT'S NOTHING PERSONAL

Question/comment from a seeker:

I'm easily provoked. When I am judged, I take it quite badly.

Epictetus' answer (*Maxims*, Of True Philosophy, 6):

Is it any use insulting a stone that cannot hear you? When people insult you, imitate a rock and ignore them.

Psychological Reflection

When someone judges us, we usually think they mean to offend us, and we take it personally.

Perhaps your boss told you that the presentation you sent them wasn't well done. But what if your boss had just gone through a bad day?

Maybe someone accuses you of always replying too late to their messages. But what if they have an 'obsessive' personality and charges everyone with the same offence?

There are so many factors that can interfere with communication between two people, that it is best not to take their judgement to heart. The next time you are criticised, remember the saying of a Hindu meditation master: if there is one fool, let's not have two.

75

WHAT YOU LEARN WITH PHILOSOPHY

Question/comment from a seeker:

Although Stoic philosophy sounds very interesting, I find it very difficult to live this way.

Epictetus' answer (*Maxims*, Of the Deceptive Opinion of Things, 23):

They say that learning philosophy takes a long time and is difficult. But it is not so, because what you learn in philosophy is to accept God's will, limit one's desires and make good use of one's reason.

Psychological Reflection

Here, Epictetus encourages us to start working on ourselves, assuring us that it is not too complex or difficult a task.

He gives us three main guidelines:

1) Embrace God's will, that is, accept the things we cannot change, and do not worry about what is not in our hands. We must be thankful and enjoy all that life lends us, and serenely let go of what it takes away from us.
2) Do not wish for too many things. Above all, as Epictetus often repeated in his lectures, we should not yearn for what is not in our control, so as to save ourselves the unhappiness when we do not get what we want.
3) We should use our reason well, think before we act, evaluate carefully before we make a decision, and use our logic so that we don't regret anything later on.

Now think of a dilemma or an issue that worries you, and put it through this triple filter. You can ask yourself:

Is the outcome or solution in my hands? If it is not, why worry about it?

Is it related to a desire? Would I be more at ease if I didn't have this yearning? If so, can I give up on it?

And finally, have I analysed the issue with a cool head, without my emotions getting the better of me?

76

YOUR PRIORITIES

Question/comment from a seeker:

Someday, when I have more time, I will dedicate myself to my personal development. I don't have time for these things right now.

Epictetus' answer (*Maxims*, Of Self-improvement, 87):

When you put off being a better person until tomorrow, it's like saying that today you want to be a person who lies, is angry, jealous or self-interested. Why not be a good person today? Go ahead, start becoming a better person right now. Don't put it off until tomorrow. If you do, you'll postpone it again on the next day.

Psychological Reflection

The Buddha is reputed to have said that our biggest problem is that we think we have a lot of time.

But everything we do or want demands a certain amount of our time ... Lose weight? Find another job? Sort out our house and our bills? 'When I have time, I'll see what I can do!'

But we all have only twenty-four hours in a day. And we live most of the day on autopilot, without stopping to think about what our priorities are and whether we spend enough time on them.

Epictetus reminds us to prioritise what is most important to us—to spend time being a good person.

When we put the most significant things first, the rest is in better order.

77

REAL HAPPINESS

Question/comment from a seeker:

How can I be truly happy forever?

Epictetus' answer (*Maxims*, Of Happiness, 1):

Real happiness must be inner happiness—stable and lasting, unaffected by everything that happens around us. If it does not meet these conditions, it is a false happiness.

Psychological Reflection

Here, the wise man seems to speak of a more mystical, spiritual happiness, rather than happiness based on material possessions or earthly riches.

Epictetus sometimes expresses thoughts similar to those found in most religions and cultures, suggesting that through spiritual practice, one can achieve a stable and lasting form of happiness—one that isn't dependent on time, external circumstances or physical conditions.

If our goal is to achieve greater 'psychological happiness' in our daily lives, it is essential that we are able to appreciate all the good that surrounds us, to know what we can contribute to the world and to be able to enjoy with little.

Moreover, we can see life as a school, where we never stop learning until the end. This point of view can also help us adopt a 'growth mindset', which is necessary for our personal development, and to be able to face our existence and its challenges with maturity.

What makes you the happiest right now?

Which level of Maslow's hierarchy of needs does your happiness correspond to: does it have to do with security, belongingness and affection, self-actualisation, or does it correspond to satisfying your spiritual or physiological needs?

Do you give more importance to the body or the soul in order to find happiness?

78

PUT IT INTO PRACTICE

Question/comment from a seeker:

I've already understood the guidelines on how to be happier and lead a better life. What's the next step?

Epictetus' answer (*Maxims*, Of Self-Improvement, 89):

I ask you what progress you have made in your personal development, and in response, you show me a valuable book you are trying to understand. That's like if I asked an athlete how fast he is, and he shows me his running shoes instead.

And just as I would like to know how fast the athlete is in those shoes, I would like to know what you have done with the knowledge in that book. Have you put its advice into practice? Do you know how to manage your desires and fears better? Our progress is always reflected in our actions.

Psychological Reflection

We are coming to the end of this book, and now, you should ask yourself: what advice from Epictetus has stuck in your memory? We tend to remember what strikes us the most or what we can relate to in our own life. Which of the guidelines did you like the most, and which ones can you put into practice, and how?

Seneca, Marcus Aurelius and Epictetus repeatedly remind us that Stoic philosophy is very practical, and we will only understand it when we begin converting wisdom into wise actions.

79

HOW TO LIVE A GOOD LIFE

Question/comment from a seeker:

If you had one last piece of advice to give me, what would it be?

Epictetus' answer (*Maxims*, Miscellaneous, 61):

Practise these maxims and obey them faithfully, as if they were laws that you must not break. Never be troubled or bothered by what others say about you, for this is one of the many things that are not in your control.

Psychological Reflection

What can you do to live a little more in accordance with this last piece of advice from Epictetus?

BIBLIOGRAPHY

Epictetus' responses were inspired by the original texts *The Enchiridion and The Handbook and Maxims*. The latter is a compilation that includes content from *The Enchiridion* along with additional discourses recorded by Epictetus' disciple.

Epictetus (1991). *Equiridión*. [*The Enchiridion*]. Barcelona: Anthropos Editorial.

Epictetus (1980). *Manual y Máximas*. [*The Handbook and Maxims*]. Ciudad de México: Editorial Porrúa, S. A.

Aurelius, M. (1985). *Meditaciones*. [*Meditations*], Madrid: Alianza Editorial S.A.

Capri, J., & Díaz, Ch. (2021). *Stay Calm with Seneca*. Barcelona: Amazon KDP.

Capri, J., & Díaz, Ch. (2020). *Stay Positive with Marcus Aurelius*. Barcelona: Amazon KDP.

Séneca, L. A. (1984). *Cartas morales a Lucilio*. [*Moral Letters to Lucilius*]. (Vol. I-II). Barcelona: Ediciones Orbis, S.A.